Which Way?

Marthe Jocelyn • Tom Slaughter

Tundra Books

For Michael
and
for Robert

Text copyright © 2010 by Marthe Jocelyn
Illustrations copyright © 2010 by Tom Slaughter

Published in Canada by Tundra Books,
75 Sherbourne Street, Toronto, Ontario M5A 2P9

Published in the United States by Tundra Books of Northern New York,
P.O. Box 1030, Plattsburgh, New York 12901

Library of Congress Control Number: 2009928992

Library and Archives Canada Cataloguing in Publication

Jocelyn, Marthe
        Which way? / Marthe Jocelyn ; Tom Slaughter, illustrator.

ISBN 978-0-88776-970-2

        1. Traffic signs and signals–Juvenile literature. 2. Street signs–Juvenile literature.
3. Travel–Juvenile literature. I. Slaughter, Tom II. Title.

TE228.J62 2010   j388.3'122   C2009-904571-0

We acknowledge the financial support of the Government of Canada through the Book Publishing Industry Development Program (BPIDP) and that of the Government of Ontario through the Ontario Media Development Corporation's Ontario Book Initiative. We further acknowledge the support of the Canada Council for the Arts and the Ontario Arts Council for our publishing program.

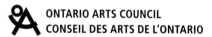 ONTARIO ARTS COUNCIL
CONSEIL DES ARTS DE L'ONTARIO

Medium: Painted paper cuts

Printed in China

1 2 3 4 5 6   15 14 13 12 11 10

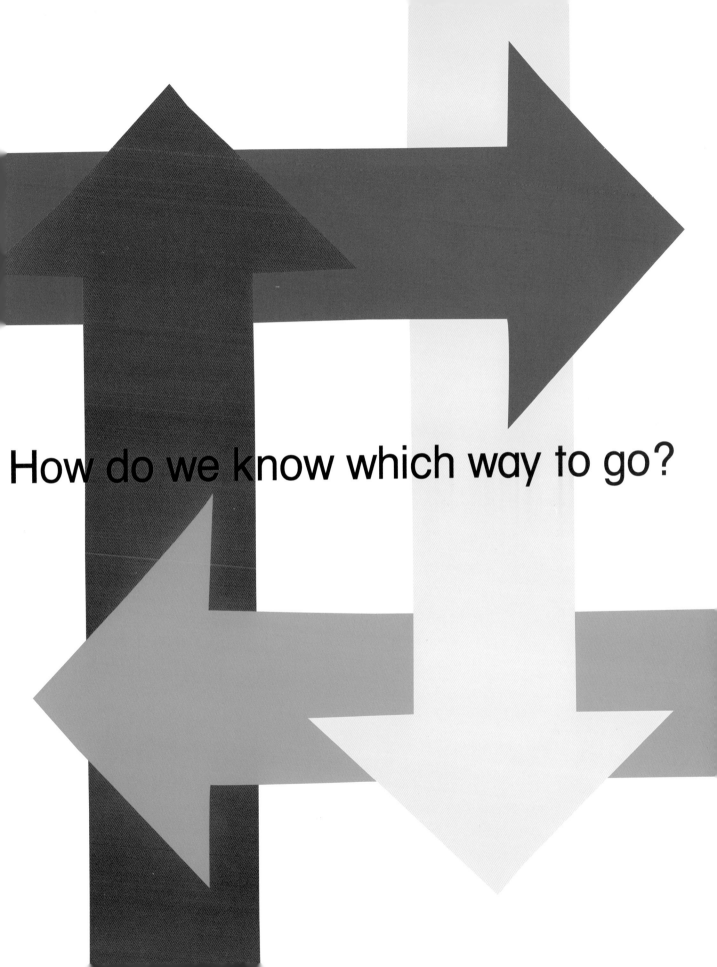

How do we know which way to go?

Will we walk or ride?
Will we pedal or drive?

Will we sail

or fly?

Will we go ONE WAY?
And get there quickly?

Or take a DETOUR
and see the scenery?

Green means go,
yellow means slow.

Red
means
to
wait
our
turn.

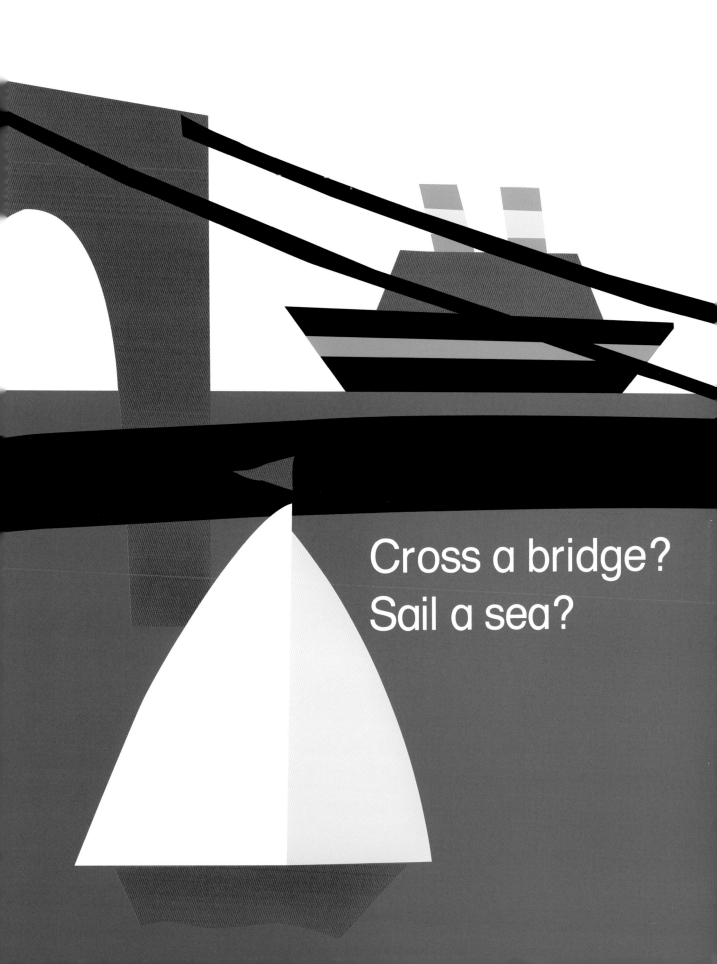

Cross a bridge?
Sail a sea?

How do we know which way to go?

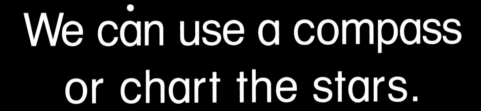

We can use a compass
or chart the stars.

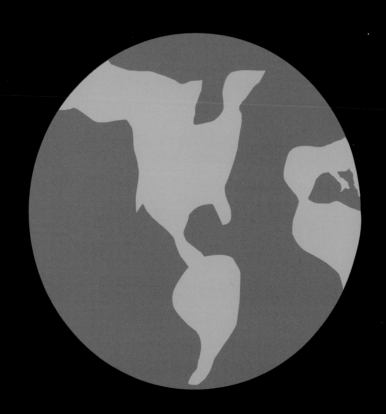

Or a map will show us
roads and rivers and towns.

We can
follow the signs.

It could be
SLIPPERY WHEN WET.

We might
see a DEER
CROSSING.

There will likely be
a BUMP or two along the way.

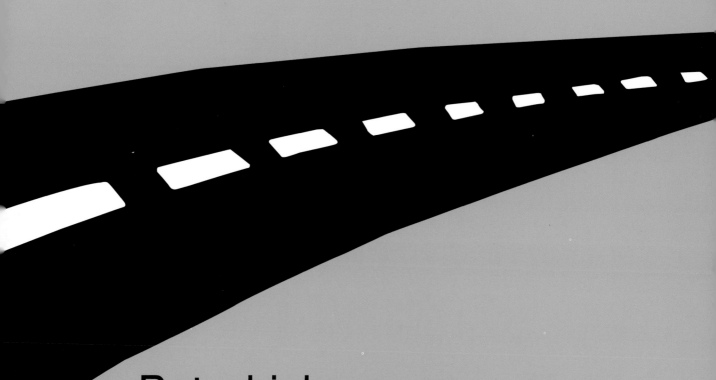

But whichever way we go,
the end of our journey
is called the destination.

And that is where we . . .

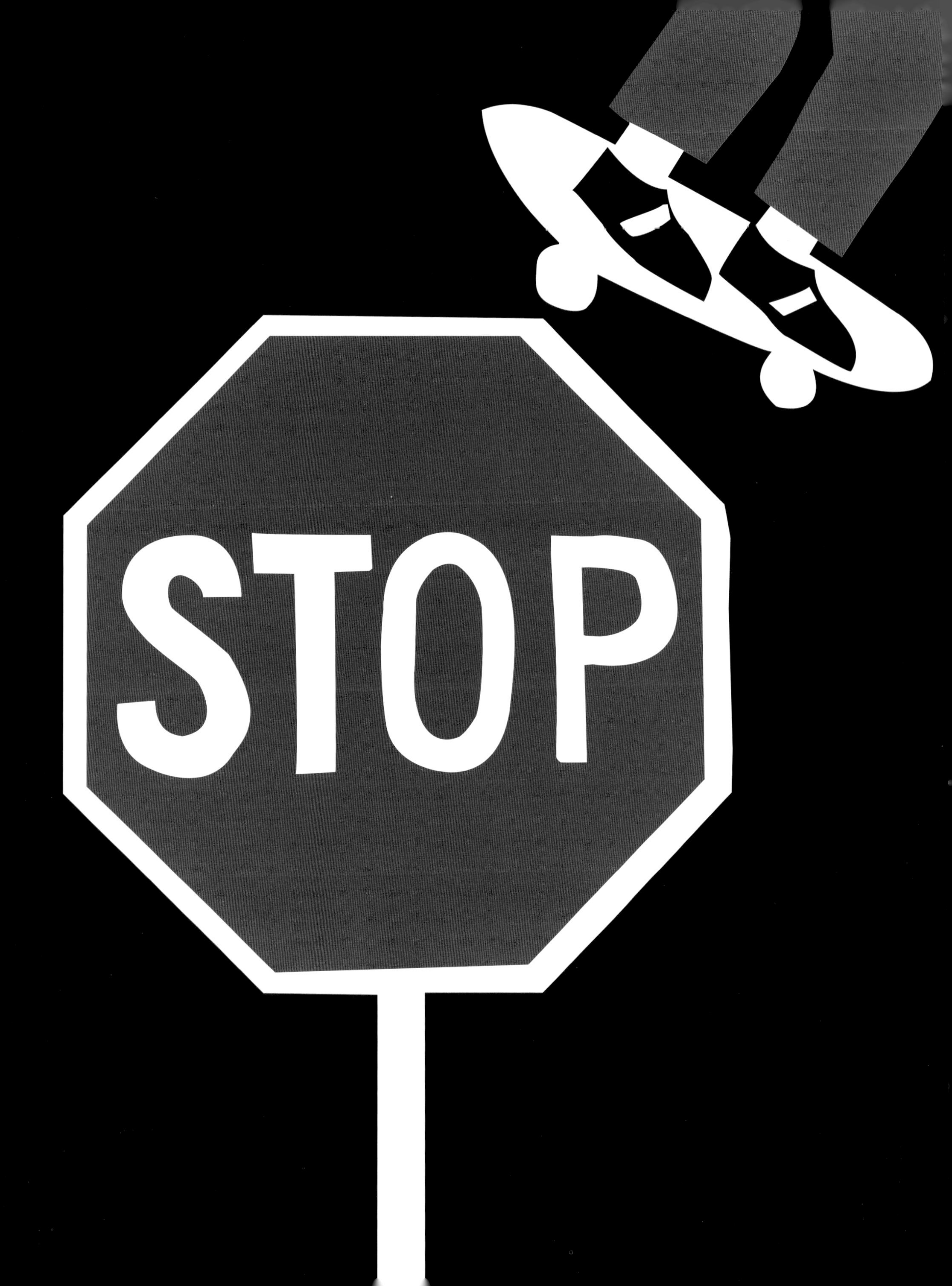
STOP